THE TOOTH BOOK

A BOOK FOR CHILDREN TO ENJOY AND LEARN ABOUT TEETH, CAVITIES, AND OTHER DENTAL HEALTH FACTS

ROUNDED SPECS
PUBLISHING
978-1-952343-04-9

Story & Art by
MARK BACERA

CO-BJF-999

This is Booth.

A few months ago, Booth lost a **tooth**.

He's been waiting and waiting, and *finally*, something should be **popping out**.

Here it is—it's finally coming out!

It's T ...

Tofu!?

No! He's been waiting
for something else!

Wait, what's this?
It's a **T** . . .

t-Turnip!?
No! He's been waiting
for something else!

Wait, what's this?
It's a **T** ...

t-t-Tapioca Milk Tea!?

No! He's been waiting
for something else!

Wait, what's this?
It's a **T** . . .

t-t-t-Tuna!?

No! He's been waiting
for something else!

Wait, what's this?
It's a **T** ...

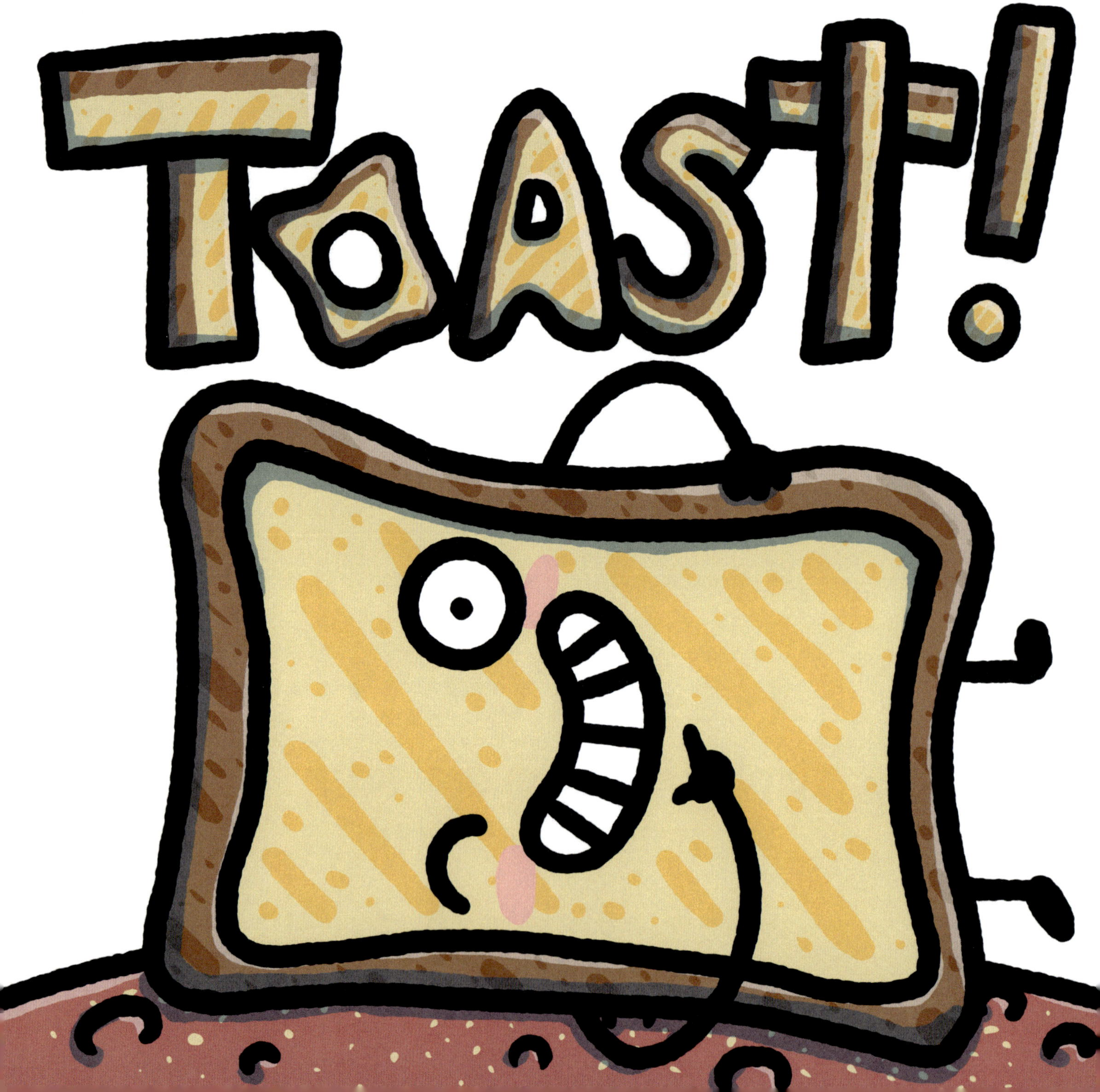
TOAST!

t-t-t-t-Toast!?

No! He's been waiting
for something else!

Wait, what's this?
It's a **T**...

t-t-t-t-t-Tomato!?

No! He's been waiting
for something else!

Wait, what's this?

It's a **T** . . .

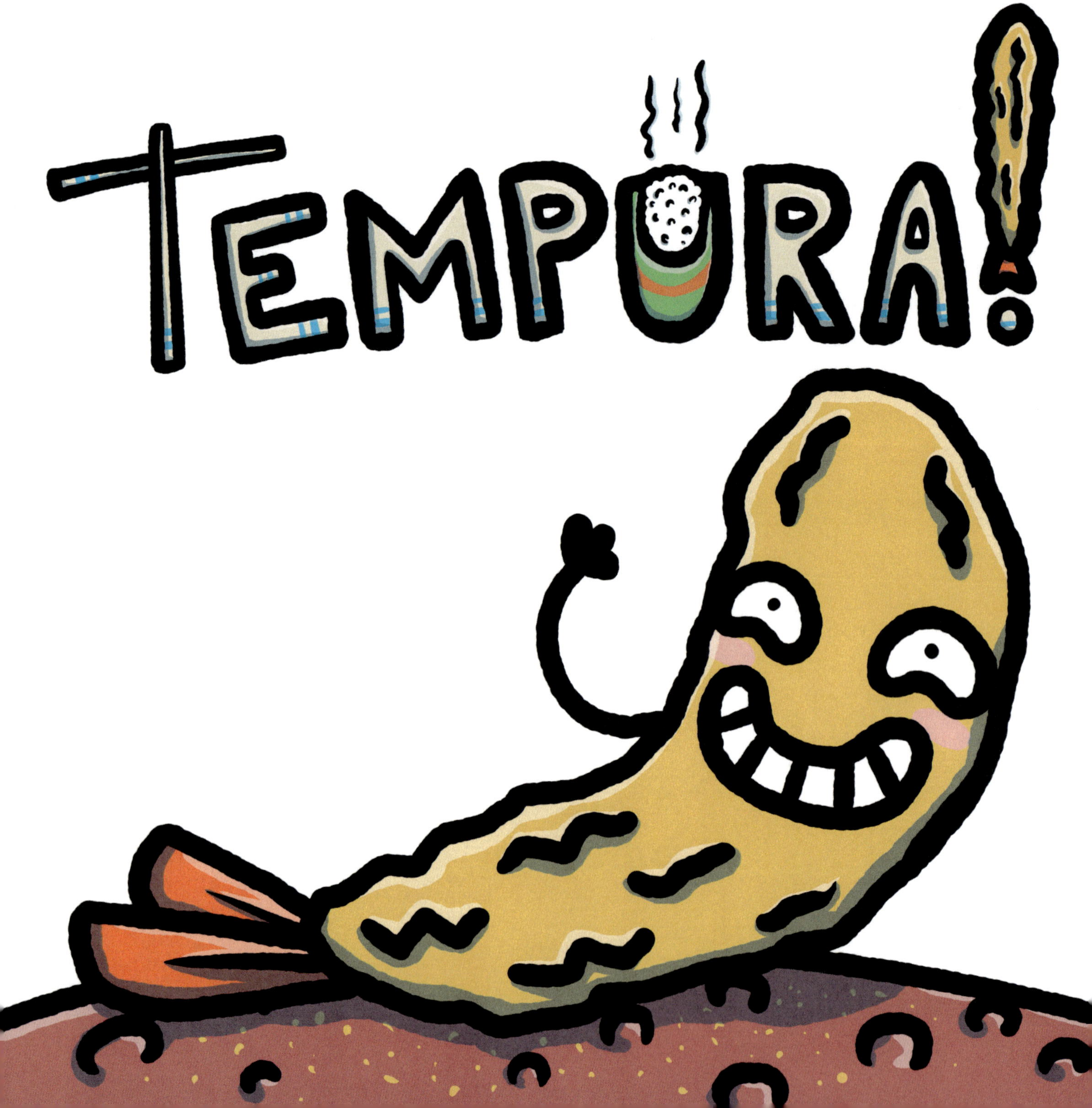
TEMPURA!

t-t-t-t-t-t-Tempura!?

No! He's been waiting
for something else!

Wait, what's this?

It's a **T**...

t-t-t-t-t-t-t-T-Bone Steak!?

No! He's been waiting
for something else!

Wait, what's this?

It's a **T** . . .

t-t-t-t-t-t-t-t-Taco!?

No! He's been waiting
for something else!

Wait, what's this?

It's a **T**...

And an adult one as well!

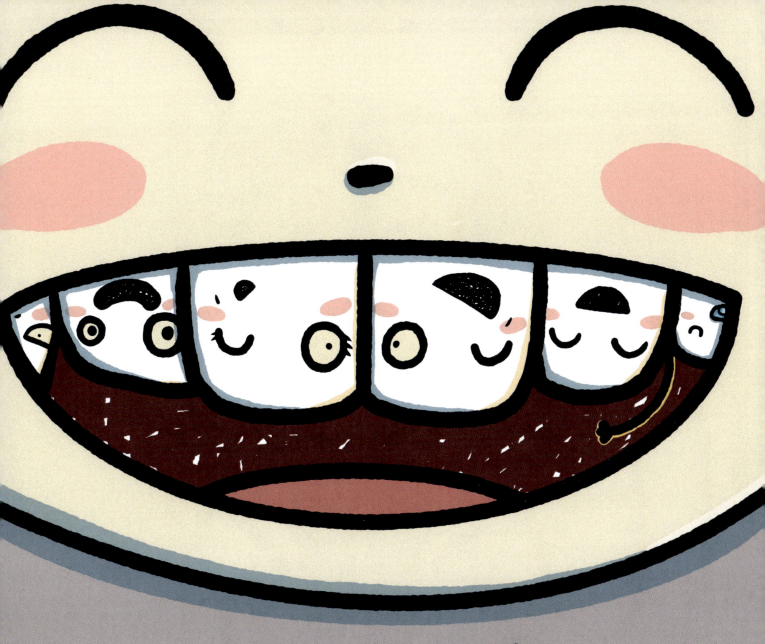

Booth got his **tooth**,
and that makes him hoot!

Look at him showing off those pearly whites!

Hi, I'm Dr. Smiles.
Did you like Booth's silly story?

Wait, you say I'm a dentist
and *not* a doctor?
Well, I went to *Doctor's School* too!

After high school, I studied for
6 more years!

So yes, I'm a doctor too!

Anyways, I'm here to teach you all about
TEETH!

Let's start by looking
at our baby teeth.

Your first teeth appear at 6-12 months. These are called primary (or baby) teeth!

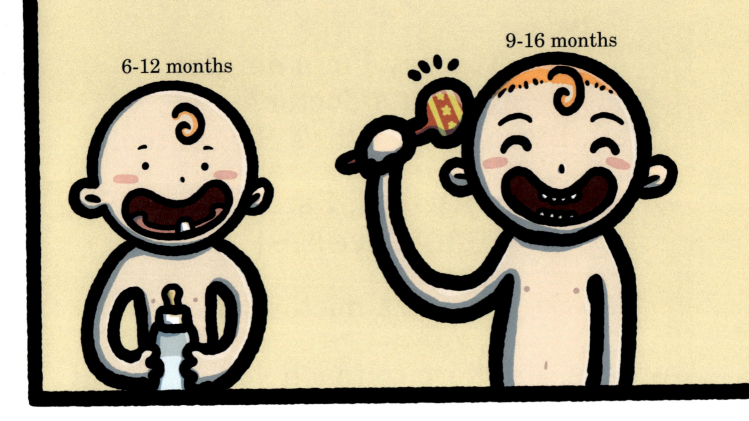

6-12 months

9-16 months

Baby teeth usually grow in order, first lower and then upper.

At 3 years old, you have a full set of 20. Then, at 5-6 years old, they start falling out.

13-19 months

23-33+ months

These numbers show the order these teeth will grow, or *erupt*.

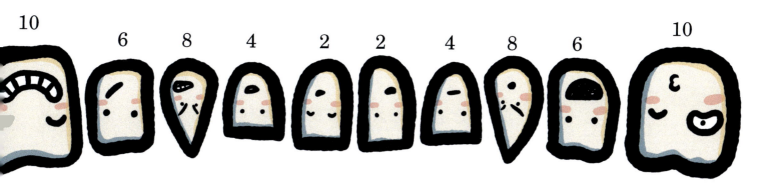

10 6 8 4 2 2 4 8 6 10

17-25 years old
(32 adult teeth)

Soon after that, your first adult, or permanent teeth start erupting. Slowly, all baby teeth are replaced by bigger and stronger teeth.

At around age 13, you'll have a full set of permanent teeth (except wisdom teeth)!

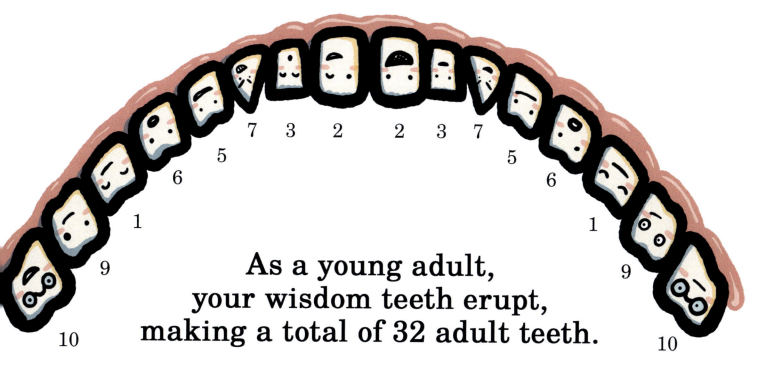

7 3 2 2 3 7

5   5

6   6

1   1

9   9

10   10

As a young adult,
your wisdom teeth erupt,
making a total of 32 adult teeth.

Adult teeth also erupt in order.

There are 5 different
types of teeth.
The first is...

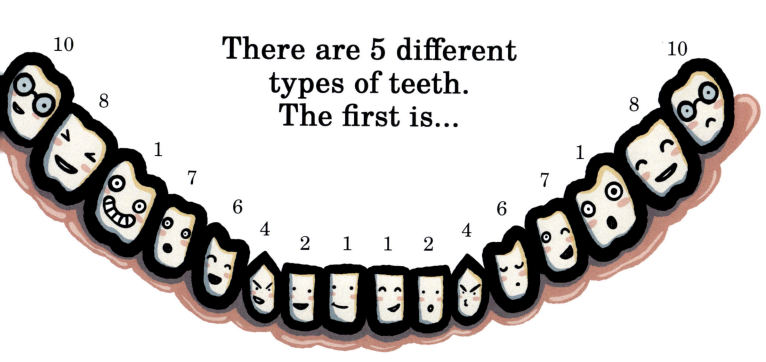

10   10

8   8

1   1

7   7

6   6

4   4

2 1 1 2

INCISORS

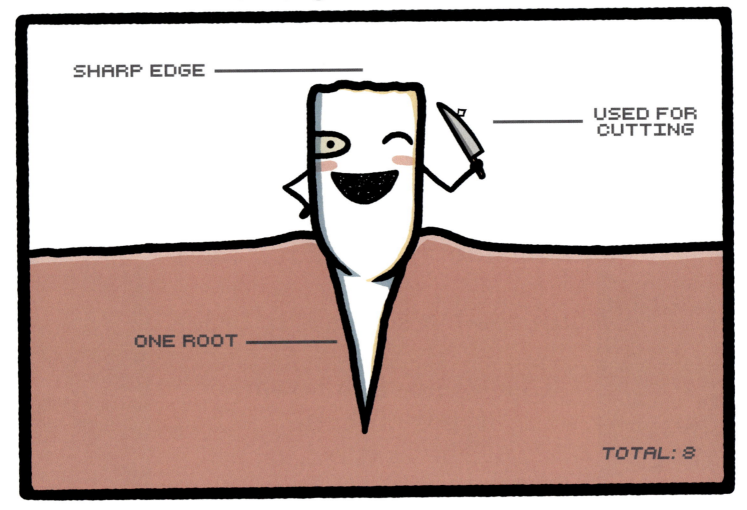

SHARP EDGE

USED FOR CUTTING

ONE ROOT

TOTAL: 8

Your 4 front teeth on each the upper and lower jaws are incisors. They have a single root and a sharp edge used to to cut food.

CANINES

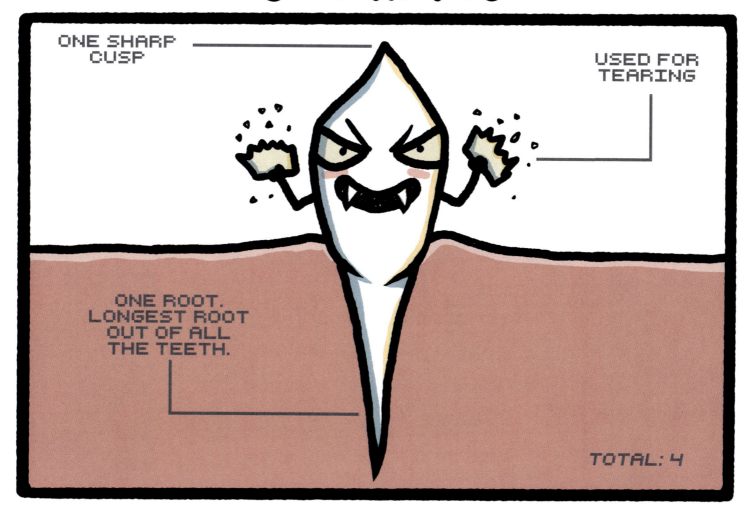

ONE SHARP CUSP

USED FOR TEARING

ONE ROOT. LONGEST ROOT OUT OF ALL THE TEETH.

TOTAL: 4

Beside your incisors are canines, 2 on the top and 2 on the bottom. They have a single root and a single pointed end called a cusp.
Canines rip and tear food.

PREMOLARS

Further back are your premolars (or bicuspids),
4 each on the bottom and top. Premolars have
1 or 2 roots and 3-4 cusps used to crush food.
Fun fact: there are no premolar baby teeth.

MOLARS

4-5 CUSPS

USED FOR GRINDING

2 OR 3 ROOTS

TOTAL: 12

Your last set of teeth is molars.
Each quadrant has 3 (including a wisdom tooth).
Some molars have 2 roots, some have 3.
Molars have a broad top surface with 4-5 cusps
used to grind food.

WISDOM TEETH

CAN SOMETIMES GROW IN WEIRD POSITIONS

SAME JOB AS OTHER MOLARS

TOTAL: 0-4

Wisdom teeth are a peculiar type of molar.
They usually erupt by the time you're 25,
but you may have any number from 0-4 of them!
Sometimes, wisdom teeth don't grow straight, cause pain,
or push other teeth and need to be removed.

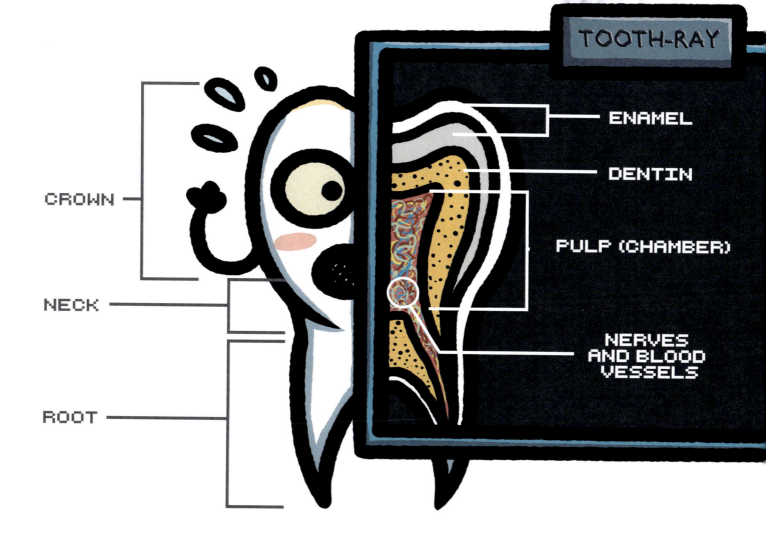

Teeth have three parts: crown, neck, and root.
The root is hidden underneath our gums.

The hard, white surface of the tooth is enamel.
It protects the tooth against decay. Below it is
dentin, which supports the enamel.

Together, enamel and dentin protect the pulp chamber,
where there are nerves and blood vessels.

Bacteria in your mouth, frequent snacking on sugary foods and drinks, and not cleaning your teeth well can end up weakening enamel and lead to the formation of a...

cavity monster

CAVITY!

This is an area in your tooth's enamel that is permanently damaged. A break or hole that goes into the dentin or pulp chamber can cause a lot of pain!

If you think you have a cavity, tell a parent and visit a dentist as soon as you can!

To fix a cavity or chipped tooth, dentists remove the decayed portion, clean the area, and fill it with a special material.

This is called a **FILLING**.

If an area in your tooth is too big for a filling, a dentist can fix it with a...

CAP or CROWN!

These are strong covers that go over the tooth. Crowns are also made out of special materials.

In the past, dentists used metals like gold and silver. Recently, however, porcelain, ceramic, and resin have become popular because of their white color.

When the crown is white, it's hard to tell a tooth even has one on!

To avoid cavities, fillings, and crowns, your best bet is to take good care of your teeth!

Brush at least twice a day for no less than two minutes each time, floss regularly, and don't forget to clean your tongue!

Remember, if you feel something strange, tell a parent and see a dentist!

The End

The Tooth Book

A Book for Children to Enjoy and Learn About Teeth, Cavities, and Other Dental Health Facts

Story and art by Mark Bacera

ISBN 978-1-952343-04-9
Copyright © 2020
Mark Bacera and Rounded Specs Publishing LLC

www.roundedspecspublishing.com
FB.me/roundedspecspublishing
Instagram: @roundedspecspublishing

About the Author

Mark Bacera is a bestselling author and released his first children's book called The Poo Poo Book (also the first book in the Bewildering Body series) in 2018. Since then, he has created several other titles.

The author lives in western Japan with his wonderful wife & daughter who also participate in the creative process and making of these books.

Amazon Author Page:
www.amazon.com/mark-bacera/e/B0198EHT0M

Email:
mark@roundedspecspublishing.com

Authors love reviews! To leave one, visit:
www.amazon.com/dp/
B08GJ13576

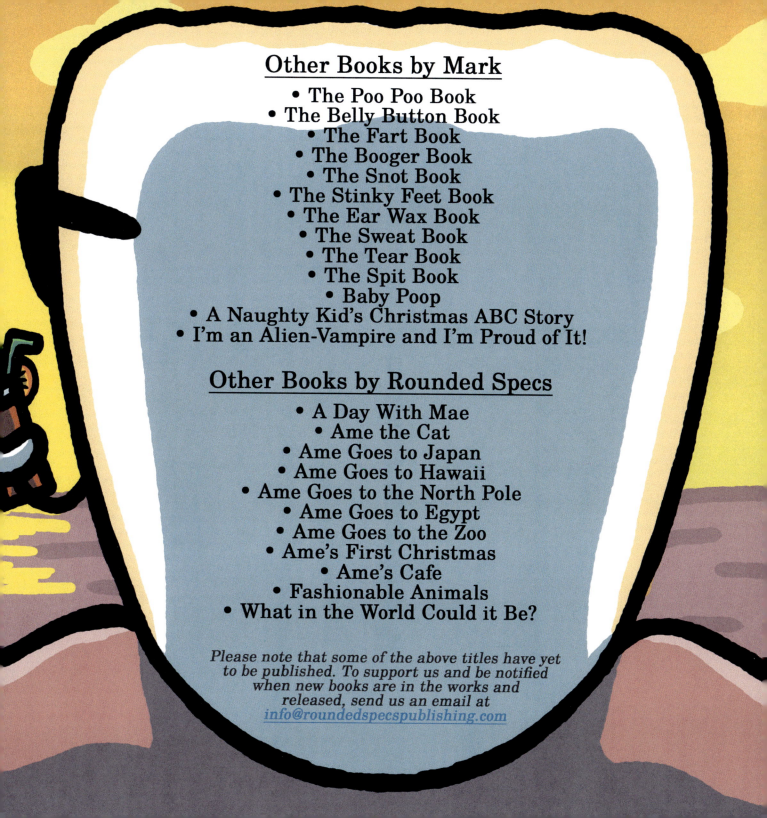

Other Books by Mark

- The Poo Poo Book
- The Belly Button Book
- The Fart Book
- The Booger Book
- The Snot Book
- The Stinky Feet Book
- The Ear Wax Book
- The Sweat Book
- The Tear Book
- The Spit Book
- Baby Poop
- A Naughty Kid's Christmas ABC Story
- I'm an Alien-Vampire and I'm Proud of It!

Other Books by Rounded Specs

- A Day With Mae
- Ame the Cat
- Ame Goes to Japan
- Ame Goes to Hawaii
- Ame Goes to the North Pole
- Ame Goes to Egypt
- Ame Goes to the Zoo
- Ame's First Christmas
- Ame's Cafe
- Fashionable Animals
- What in the World Could it Be?

Please note that some of the above titles have yet to be published. To support us and be notified when new books are in the works and released, send us an email at
info@roundedspecspublishing.com

Made in the USA
Middletown, DE
19 April 2023